LIFE SKILLS

Be smart, stay safe

Louise Spilsbury

Heinemann Library
Chicago, Illinois

www.heinemannraintree.com
Visit our website to find out
more information about
Heinemann-Raintree books.

To order:
☎ Phone 888-454-2279
🖥 Visit www.heinemannraintree.com
to browse our catalog and order online.

© 2009 Heinemann Library
an imprint of Capstone Global Library, LLC
Chicago, Illinois

Customer Service: 888-454-2279

Visit our website at
www.heinemannraintree.com

Edited by Harriet Milles and Adam Miller
Designed by Philippa Jenkins and Artistix
Picture research by Elizabeth Alexander
Production by Victoria Fitzgerald

Printed and bound in China by South China
  Printing Company Ltd.

13 12 11 10 09
10 9 8 7 6 5 4 3 2 1

**Library of Congress Cataloging-in-Publication
Data**
Spilsbury, Louise.
  Be smart, stay safe / Louise Spilsbury.
    p. cm. -- (Life skills)
  Includes bibliographical references and index.
  ISBN 978-1-4329-2724-0 (hc)
  1. Risk-taking (Psychology) 2. Adolescent
psychology. 3. Teenagers. I. Title.
  BF637.R57S75 2009
  155.5'18--dc22
                        2008047825

Acknowledgments
The author and publishers are grateful to the
following for permission to reproduce copyright
material: © Alamy pp. 23 (Andrew Paterson), 20
(Andry A/Alamsyah), 16 (Blend Images/Dave &
Les Jacobs), 40 (Jupiterimages/ BananaStock), 30
(Tony French), 11 (Zak Waters); © Barcroft
Media p. 35; © Corbis pp. 14 (Flirt/Ariel
Skelley), 29 (Kevin Dodge), 5 (Thinkstock);
© Getty Images/Taxi/Carl Schneider p. 7;
© Iofoto/Dreamstime.com p. 33; © iStockphoto
pp. 13 (Carsten Madsen), 26 (Paige Falk);
© Masterfile pp. 22 (Peter Griffith), 25 (Ron
Fehling); © Photolibrary pp. 43 (Digital Vision),
45 (Index Stock Imagery/Donald Higgs); © Rex
Features/Oliver Grove/PYMCA p. 39; © Science
Photo Library pp. 49 (AJ Photo), 47 (Faye
Norman); © Shutterstock pp. 19 (Arland
Croquet), 9 (Andrija Kovac), 36 (Jose AS Reyes).

Cover photograph of a teenage girl with a laptop
computer and cell phone reproduced with
permission of © Shutterstock/David Davis.

We would like to thank Robin Lomas for his
invaluable help in the preparation of this book.

Every effort has been made to contact copyright
holders of material reproduced in this book.
Any omissions will be rectified in subsequent
printings if notice is given to the publishers.

Contents

Some words are printed in bold, **like this**. You can find out what they mean by looking in the glossary.

Taking Risks

News headlines often highlight the problems of risk-taking teenagers. They usually focus on the trouble teenagers cause for other people, such as **vandalism** or late-night noise. Sometimes they mention the damage teenagers do to themselves, such as sustaining injuries from driving recklessly or missing out on an education because they skip school. But is it always bad to take risks?

POSITIVE RISK-TAKING

Taking risks is an inevitable and important part of teenage life. As a teenager you are much more independent—you are out on your own more, making your own friends, trying new things and new experiences. Increased independence means more choices, and of course that means more risks. This is not necessarily a bad thing. People need to take on new challenges to figure out who they are and what they can and want to be.

Taking risks can be a good thing when it means trying a new challenge. This could be something you have wanted to do for a long time but didn't dare to do, such as playing a solo at a concert or running a race. Alternatively, it could be trying a totally new sport or joining a club to make new friends. Healthy risk-taking is anything that puts you in a difficult or unfamiliar situation. It may involve the possibility of failure, but it also gives you the chance to have positive experiences and gain a new belief in yourself. Taking risks like this gives you a real rush as your adrenalin kicks in, whether you succeed or fail in your goals.

Negative risk-taking

Negative risk-taking is anything that puts you or someone else at risk of being hurt or damaged. Such damage could be emotional or physical. Negative risky behaviors range from going on a blind date with someone you met online or drinking at parties, to doing your own body piercings or carrying a weapon.

Most of the time, and for most people, even these risky behaviors will not result in disaster, but sometimes negative risk-taking has deadly consequences. The number of accidental deaths caused by fighting, driving too fast, or just fooling around dangerously is highest in males 16 to 25 years old.

When people get up on stage to perform, they take a big risk. They face the fear that they might be laughed off or that people simply won't like what they do. It takes a lot of guts to take risks like these—far more so than a lot of the negative risks people take.

There are many ways you can take positive new risks, including:

- Joining a band, club, or group
- Trying rollerblading, rock climbing, or sailing
- Taking an extra class in a school subject you find difficult
- Trying out for a sports team
- Auditioning for a school play
- Running for student council
- Volunteering to help out for a worthy cause, such as at an animal shelter, at a home for the elderly, or for an environmental organization.

Why take risks?

What motivates one person to take more risks than another depends on the individual. Some people have a stronger drive to feel different from their **peers**, and some are more susceptible to peer pressure than others.

For some people, just being around friends makes them more likely to take risks. Others end up taking more risks because they make decisions based purely on what is happening at that moment without thinking about how it might affect themselves, other people, or the world around them.

Which risks are real?

It can be tough deciding which risks are real and which are not. You may think that parents and caregivers overexaggerate risks. It is true that this can sometimes happen, but it is usually because they love you and want to protect you.

In order to stop your parents' or caregivers' fears from restricting the positive risks you take, talk things through with them first. Find out if their fears are based on facts, or whether they are based on media hype. They will be impressed that you are mature enough to be willing to discuss it properly. Faced with the facts, they are more likely to give you more freedom.

There are some activities, such as white-water rafting or sky-diving, that carry a certain degree of real risk, but that does not necessarily mean you should never try them. The risks are greatly reduced if you choose to do these things with a company or organization that follows strict safety guidelines and has a great safety record. Taking steps to keep the real risks to a minimum will be reassuring for you and your family.

Get it in perspective

Thinking about risks is not about trying to scare yourself. In reality, the likelihood of something bad happening to you is pretty low. However, taking chances and making the wrong choices in a situation obviously puts you at greater risk, so it is best to think ahead and take precautions to keep yourself, your possessions, and your friends and others safe.

When you learn how to evaluate risks and anticipate the consequences of your choices, you will be safer and more able to cope with challenges in all parts of your adult life.

White-water rafting does involve some risk-taking—but very few people who have tried it have regretted the experience!

At the age of 14, **entrepreneur** Nick Bell set up an online teen magazine and sold it two years later for almost $1.5 million. He has since bought back the company and set up a number of other successful websites. Nick says: "I tell people who have an idea to go for it and follow their instincts. I suppose I am living proof that you can be successful. I have taken risks but if you have a dream I think you have to follow it."

Getting it Right

PLAY IT SAFE

It may be the last thing you want to think about when planning a weekend or a night out, but taking unnecessary risks at parties or concerts, when playing sports, or at the beach is a surefire way to put a damper on things. Taking a few simple precautions can make the difference between having a great weekend or one that you'd rather forget!

PARTY TIME

At parties or some clubs, one of the greatest dangers you will face is alcohol. It is tempting to think that drinking alcohol will give you more confidence and help you feel relaxed. Some people see their parents or other adults drinking and believe that it is a "socially acceptable" drug. They feel confident that they know and can set their own limits. In fact, alcohol has a far stronger effect on a young person's body than it does on an adult's. This means that you will lose control far more quickly on far fewer drinks.

Studies have shown that the younger people start drinking, the more likely they are to develop problems with alcohol—with serious implications for health. Even moderate drinking can cause short- and long-term damage to a young, growing brain. Longer-term risks from alcohol include **cancer**, high blood pressure, and liver disease.

Drinking alcohol clouds your judgment and makes you do embarrassing, stupid, or dangerous things that you regret the next day. If you drink alcohol, you are far more likely to do something dangerous or violent, such as getting into a fight or driving when drunk. You may even be taken advantage of in a way that you can never undo—for instance, having underage and unprotected sex.

Getting it Right

If you are at a party where a lot of people are drinking alcohol, the safest thing to do would be to leave. If that is not possible, pour your own drinks so you can be sure nobody has spiked them with alcohol. Never leave your drink unattended, in case someone spikes it when you are not looking. Stay among groups of people you know and trust.

Turn down the volume

Another serious risk for partygoers is NOISE! Have you ever gotten back from a night out and felt that ringing in your ears or a dulled sense of hearing? Any sustained loud noise puts a person's hearing at risk, and the **decibel levels** in a club can be as bad as standing near a jackhammer. Hearing damage is caused by two factors: the volume at which you listen to it, and how long you listen to it.

Try the following tips and you will be able to give your ears a break but still enjoy the music:

• If you are at a music festival or club, take a break somewhere quiet to give your ears a rest.

• Never stand too close to loudspeakers.

• If you want to watch the main act at the front of the stage, watch the opening bands from further back.

Avoid dancing or standing next to loudspeakers because your ears will suffer.

SPORTS

Playing sports or getting some other form of regular exercise will keep you in good shape. However, there is some potential for injuries in sports. There are many things you can do to keep yourself injury-free. Start by learning the rules of the game; they are there to make games fair and to keep players safe. Knowing the rules means that you are prepared, so you will not be caught off guard. For example, in soccer it is against the rules to kick a ball after the referee's whistle has blown, because an unexpected tackle could cause serious injuries.

Be properly equipped

One of the main reasons people get injured during sports is because they use the wrong or badly fitting equipment. Save your smile by wearing mouth guards for fast-moving sports such as football and hockey. Wear elbow, wrist, and knee guards to prevent bone fractures when skating or skateboarding. A helmet will protect your head when you are up to bat in baseball.

Wearing the right shoes can stop you from falling and injuring yourself, and will also improve your play. If you want to try extreme sports, make sure you take all the right precautions, wear all the correct safety gear, and have a qualified instructor who can use his or her skills and experience to control the risks.

Warm up, cool down

Before you get out on the field and involved in the action, it is important to do a **warm-up**, such as jogging in place or stretching. Warm-ups prepare your heart for an increase in activity and increase the blood flow to the muscles, making them warmer and more elastic (ready to move). Cold muscles do not absorb shock or impact as well and are more easily **strained** or pulled. Doing some gentle walking or stretching exercises after sports also helps to relax your muscles and prevent soreness. This is known as a **cool-down**.

Getting it Right

If you feel the need to take on physically challenging risks, you should sign up for a class or join an organization where you can test your limits in a relatively safe environment. You could try rock climbing, surfing, or white-water rafting.

Controlling risks by using the proper equipment makes the difference between taking part in a real sport and plain dangerous behavior.

Pain is the body's way of telling you something is wrong, so:

- Never play sports when you are injured or in pain.

- Never play when you have a cold or flu bug or are sick in some other way.

- Don't take pain relievers to get you through a game.

- Don't return to a sport before you are fully healed after an injury.

VACATION HIGHS AND LOWS

It is great to go on a summer trip with friends—mountain biking, camping in the woods, or visiting the beach to swim or surf—but be alert for risks. This is particularly important by the ocean. Unfortunately, every year people are killed after being swept out on inflatables, or surfing too far out to sea with no understanding of currents, or being trapped on a beach when the high tide comes in.

When camping, take warm clothing and sleeping bags, because in most places the temperature drops dramatically at night. If you light a campfire, build it in a shallow pit away from the tent and anything else that might catch on fire, and surround it with rocks. Keep a bucket of water nearby and use this to put out the fire. Embers can stay hot enough to reignite or burn skin for up to a day if a fire is only covered with sand.

Sun sense

Up to 80 percent of teenagers put themselves at risk by failing to use a sunscreen lotion. Sun damage to the skin in your youth can make your skin patchy and wrinkled in later life, and even lead to skin cancers. Doctors advise that sunscreens should be applied just before going out in the sun and reapplied frequently throughout the day, particularly after swimming. You should also cover up exposed areas such as the head, arms, and legs in hats and clothing made of light-colored fabrics.

When you are camping or hiking:

- **Take first-aid supplies and plenty of drinking water. Stream or river water may be unsafe.**

- **Carry a cell phone or find out where the nearest telephone is located.**

- **Check the weather forecast before you leave.**

- **Pack essentials, such as a flashlight, extra food, water, and rain gear, even if it looks sunny.**

- **Tell people where you are going, who is with you, and when you will return.**

- **Follow well-marked trails and do not stray from the route.**

Getting it
Wrong

Sometimes people take the risk of jumping into water from high cliffs, walls, and piers. Several people have died doing this, either drowning or crashing into rocks. In 2008 Steven Andrews, 25, was paralyzed from the neck down after jumping 26 feet (8 meters) into just 3 feet (1 meter) of water. He said: "I want to warn people that you should never mess around on rocks or cliffs or anywhere dangerous near water. It can happen so quickly—in a matter of seconds my life changed forever. I wish I could turn back the clock but now I'm just going to have to try and deal with it."

WORKWISE

Having a part-time job is great because it gives you cash of your own to spend. It also gives you the chance to try a few different jobs before you get out into the world of full-time work. However, every year tens of thousands of teenage employees end up in the emergency room with injuries sustained through unsafe equipment or conditions at their workplace (for instance, slippery floors). These accidents tend to happen when young people are working too fast or for too long, or when they have not been given proper safety training or **supervision**.

Keep it legal

Most countries have laws to protect young people at work. In the United States, these vary somewhat from state to state. These laws prevent you from taking on dangerous jobs, or jobs for which you have not been properly trained. The laws also restrict the number of hours that young people can work. This is mainly to ensure that, at this important age, you have time for your studies and to relax and get the sleep that you need.

Check out how the law affects you before you agree to start any new job. Always discuss a job with your parents or caregivers first to make sure they are comfortable with you doing it.

To be safe at work:

- Follow all the safety rules.

- Use safety equipment and wear protective clothing when needed.

- Keep work areas clean and organized.

- Know what to do in an emergency.

- Report any health and safety hazards to your supervisor.

One of the most important things you can do to reduce the risks at work is to have the confidence to speak up if you are unhappy about something you are being asked to do.

QUIZ
HOW SAFETY SAVVY ARE YOU?

Are you in the know, or too irresponsible to be let out alone? Find out in this true or false quiz. The answers are on page 50.

1) Some music just has to be listened to at maximum volume.
2) You only need safety gear for a sport if you are a professional.
3) During the school week, 14- and 15-year-olds can do a maximum of three hours of work a day.
4) When school is not in session, 14- and 15-year-olds can work up to eight hours a day.
5) Red and yellow flags mean it is safe to swim on a beach.
6) It is safe to swim in polluted water, as long as you don't swallow any of it.
7) You should stay out of the sun in the afternoon.
8) It is okay to swim alone as long as you are a strong swimmer.
9) In sports, a warm-up is a drink of hot chocolate after a winter game.

Be Streetwise

The risks of having an accident or being mugged or attacked while you are out in the streets are low, but it is wise to think ahead and avoid potential dangers. When you go out at night, it is especially important to know how you can get home safely at the end of the evening.

PLAN AHEAD

You never want to end up hitchhiking or getting rides from strangers, as these options are far too risky. Always arrange to get a ride from a responsible person, catch a bus or train, take a taxi, or stay at a friend's house. Another important thing to remember is to tell your family where you are going, when you plan to be back, and the route you intend to take.

If strangers stop to ask for your help or offer you a ride, keep your distance and never get into a car with them—no matter their sex, and no matter how friendly they seem. If they harass or scare you, shout clearly "Help me!" or "Call the police."

Alternatively, agree to text or call parents or caregivers before you head for home, so that they know when to expect you. If you don't have a safe ride home, call your parents. Even if it is late, they would rather you called so that they can make sure you get home safely, rather than let you take risks.

Road safety

Car crashes are the biggest single cause of accidental death for 12- to 16-year-olds in the United States. Teenagers have the lowest rate of seat belt use and the highest crash rate compared to other age groups. They are more likely to be in a car accident and less likely to be using a seat belt when it happens. Teenagers are involved with more accidents because they or their friends are inexperienced drivers and because teen drivers are more likely to speed and drive dangerously when they are with friends. Drivers 17 years old are 39 percent more likely be killed with one passenger than when alone and 86 percent more at risk with two passengers. To keep safe, simply belt up and choose whom you ride with carefully.

"Drunk driving is the nation's most frequently committed violent crime. . . . Underage drinking is the No. 1 youth drug problem."

Glynn Birch, president of Mothers Against Drunk Driving (MADD)

CYCLE SAFETY

Cycling is a great way to travel independently. It is also a cheap form of transportation, keeps you fit, gets you out in the fresh air, and is environmentally friendly because it reduces the amount of fuel-driven traffic on the road. The benefits of cycling far outweigh the risks, but it pays to be aware of the risks.

Get the gear

One of the simplest things you can do to keep safe on your bike is wear a helmet. OK, so no one likes helmet hair, but the alternative could be far more depressing: around three-quarters of people killed in cycling accidents die from major head injuries.

You might want to invest in a pair of cycling gloves, as these help you to grip the handlebars and protect your knuckles if you fall. However, what is even more important is making sure that you can be seen. Wear high-visibility clothing such as an over-the-shoulder-style **reflective** belt.

Rules of the road

Many accidents involving bikes and cars happen at intersections, where cyclists may not be sure of the rules of the road or take unnecessary risks. It is a good idea to take a course in cycle safety, as this will improve your safety awareness and your confidence. Make sure you know the rules of the road.

When you cycle, especially in a city, be smart:

- Never cycle in places that are too dangerous to walk in.
- Use a cycle lane when you can; otherwise keep on the inside of traffic without getting too close to the curb or road edge.
- Keep well behind trucks or large vehicles so that drivers can see you clearly in their rearview mirrors.
- Watch the road. Manholes, potholes, and litter can send you off course. On busy streets, watch for people in parked cars opening their doors.
- Lock your bike securely whenever you leave it.

By checking your bike regularly for problems and keeping it in good condition, you can reduce the chances of having an accident or breakdown. For example, you should keep the chain clean and oiled, check the brakes and brake cables, and make sure your tires are pumped up and that the wheels run smoothly when they spin. Caring for your bike will make it last longer, and it should only take you about an hour or two a month.

In dim light or rain, cyclists are almost invisible to drivers. The only way to be seen clearly is to wear reflector bands and use both front and rear lights.

DON'T BE A VICTIM!

The risk of being mugged or attacked is pretty low, but there are a number of things you can do to keep yourself safe on the streets. Simple precautions include traveling with a friend and keeping to well-lit main roads when you have to walk somewhere. It is also best to avoid deserted and wooded or bushy areas if you can, and to resist the temptation of taking shortcuts through alleyways or across dark parking lots, where people can lurk unseen.

Protect your possessions

It is also important to protect your possessions when you are out and about. One simple option is to only take a small amount of cash with you and reduce the number of valuable goods that you carry. Try not to have items such as cell phones or MP3 players on display. Keep them in a pocket. Cover any valuable jewelry with a scarf.

If someone does grab your bag or demand your valuables, give the valuables up rather than fighting to keep them. Your things can be replaced, and it is not worth taking the risk of being hurt, or worse. If you are scared or attacked, shout about it. Don't be shy—screaming can scare off an attacker and get help fast.

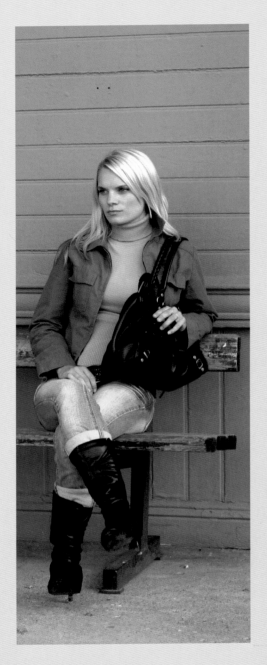

Protect your possessions by carrying your bag close to your body and facing toward you, with the fastenings closed.

To keep safe on the streets:

- Stay alert. Be aware of what's going on around you and keep your eyes and ears open. Talking on the phone or listening to an MP3 player as you walk is not a good idea.

- Trust your instincts. If you feel that something isn't safe, you are probably right.

- If you think someone is following you, go straight into a store and tell someone working there.

QUIZ   HOW STREETWISE ARE YOU?

Take this quiz, then turn to page 50 to see if you are streetwise or street-simple!

1) **When walking down a street alone, do you:**
   a) Keep to well-lit roads and avoid quiet streets, alleys, or shortcuts and set your cell to silent or vibrating so you don't attract attention if it goes off.
   b) Try to look confident and walk quickly with your head up.
   c) Put in your headphones and listen to music?

2) **If there is no cycle lane, the safest lane to ride in is:**
   a) The right lane, with the flow of traffic; b) The left lane; c) The middle of the street.

3) **At a party you meet some people who you get along really well with, so when one of them offers you a ride home, do you:**
   a) Say thanks, but explain that you have already have a ride.
   b) Say yes, but tell one of your friends who you have gone with.
   c) Say yes, because it will save you money?

4) **When you are cycling along a road and want to take a left turn, what is the first thing you do?**
   a) Look behind you at the traffic.
   b) Put your arm out to indicate you plan to turn.
   c) Brake to slow down.

Safe Surfing

Going online can be both useful and fun. It is a great way to find information quickly, talk with people around the world, download music and movies, and much more. But the Internet can have a downside. For example, you can be duped by **chatroom** liars, have your personal details stolen and abused, or receive unwanted and nasty emails or texts. Reduce the risk of Internet abuse by getting cyber-savvy.

Pick and Choose

There are some great websites out there, but there is also a lot of junk. When you search for homework help, just remember that not all sites are reliable and that any facts you find should be checked against a reliable source before you use them. When you use a search engine, you also risk opening up sites with offensive or pornographic material. You can configure your computer to filter out these types of sites and report any you find to your **Internet service provider (ISP)**.

Catching a virus

Viruses are computer programs that are deliberately designed to cause problems for computer users. At worst, they can wreck your computer. **Spyware** programs are not viruses, but they can be a nuisance when they get into your system. They may cause you to be inundated by annoying pop-up ads, or even allow someone else to take control of your computer.

These problem programs can arrive via email, **instant messenger (IM)**, your Internet connection, or even your web browser if you visit the wrong website. Protect your computer from unwanted invaders by buying or downloading good anti-virus and anti-spyware software, and be sure to update it regularly.

Getting it Wrong

There are **copyright** laws that protect images, song files, and other information, so make sure that you do not illegally use, post, share, or distribute stuff you find or download on the Internet. This goes for schoolwork, too. You can get into serious trouble for **plagiarism**, which is copying and pasting large blocks of text from the Internet and trying to pass it off as your own work!

Getting it Right

Setting up a **blog** site is a great way to share your thoughts and opinions with your friends. However, make sure that is all you share by following these tips:

- Protect the blog with a password, so that only the people you invite can access the site.

- On a public blog, never publish photos of yourself or your friends.

- Never give out personal information about yourself or your friends—for instance, your home address, the name of your school, or your cell phone number.

Most of us cannot imagine life without the Internet. But be aware that it can also open the door to offensive, threatening, or unwanted sites or people.

In the chatroom

Chatting with people online can be a great way to spend time, but talking to people you cannot see also has real risks because it is easy for people to lie. Sometimes this is a white lie—for example, when people brag that they have a better job than they do in real life. However, sometimes it is more serious—for example, when a 40-year-old creep passes himself off as an attractive 15-year-old boy to a lonely girl.

Simple systems

There are a number of basic things you can do to weed out the creeps in a chatroom. Find out about the privacy settings on Facebook, MySpace, and other social networking sites before signing up. Once you are in a chatroom, keep your messages public. Only join a private chatroom with people you already know, because if you join with strangers it is easier for them to hassle you.

Finally, never give out photos or any personal details to anyone you do not already know in real life, in case they try to trace you. Whatever online contacts might say to you, or however friendly they may seem, in reality you do not know anything for certain about them, so keep your distance. It is also a good idea to use a chatroom nickname that is different from your screen name so that cyber predators cannot track you down easily.

Take control

One of the great things about online chatting is that you are totally in control. It might be hard to escape an annoying person in the classroom, but if you do not like what someone is saying online, you can simply log off. If someone says something you think is really strange or makes you feel uncomfortable, then you should also tell your parents or the chatroom moderator. You could be saving not only yourself but also someone else a lot of trouble in the future.

Getting it Right

Never arrange to meet anyone whom you chat with on the Internet in person. Meeting someone you have only been in touch with online can be very dangerous. If you really feel you want to risk a meeting, then for your own safety you must tell a parent or caregiver—and take that person or friends with you to the meeting. Always insist that you meet in the daytime in a busy public place, such as a shopping center. If your online contact tries to persuade you not to do this, cancel the meeting— fast!

Anyone can become a victim of online deception. It has nothing to do with being easy to fool—and both girls and boys are targets. Online con artists can be very clever, so be very careful.

Getting it Wrong

In 2008 a 31-year-old Belgian man named Duval struck up a conversation with a 13-year-old teenage girl in a chatroom. After more than 3,000 emails and many cell phone calls, Duval flew to Montreal, Canada, and invited his victim to meet with him in his hotel. When the girl went missing, her parents called the police. After checking her computer and reading her emails, the police tracked the pair down at Duval's hotel room. She had a lucky escape, but many girls and boys have not been so lucky.

Cyber bullying

Cyber bullying is when someone uses email, instant messaging, chat rooms, or blogs to insult or threaten people, spread rumors about them, or otherwise deliberately upset them. This type of bullying can affect someone not just at school, but anywhere and at any time.

Some cyber bullies may not realize what harm they are doing. They may think that sending stupid messages, or that posting gossip, facts, or photos of people without asking them is just a big joke.

The fact is that uploaded information is out there for everyone to see, and the victim of the "joke" may find it anything but funny. And remember that giving out information about someone's private identity, thus making it available to strangers, is not only wrong but also dangerous.

Don't bottle things up. If you are being bullied, the first thing to do is talk to someone—a parent or caregiver, a teacher at your school, or an aunt or uncle. Other people will be able to help you make it stop.

Bullies are usually cowards. By blocking their number or posting things on a website anonymously or from an unknown location, they think they can hide who they are. However, there are a number of ways that you can use technology to fight cyber bullies.

- If you are getting problem text messages, tell your cell phone company or your Internet service provider about the bullying. They may be able to track the bully down.

- Use blocking software. You can block instant messages from certain people or use mail filters to block emails from specific email addresses. (See the TIP box below.)

- Log into a chatroom with a different user ID or nickname so the bully won't know who you are.

- Change your cell phone number and only give it out to friends you trust.

What to do about cyber bullying

If you are suffering from cyber bullying, one thing you should *not* do is reply to bullying text messages or emails, because this could make matters worse. If you don't respond, the bully is likely to get bored and move on.

If the bullying continues, save or copy and paste into a Word file any nasty emails, voicemails, or things posted on your profile, so you can use them as proof. This evidence can be used to catch the bully and stop him or her. If the bullying persists for too long or escalates to physical threats, you should also notify the police.

To block messages from a particular person on your computer:

1. Click on the person's name in the contact list to open a range of options: one of these is "Block."

2. Click on "Block," and you should not receive messages from this person anymore.

(Block is sometimes called "Ignore," and if just clicking on it doesn't work, take a look in your Preferences, or see if there is a "Block/Ignore" button in the chatroom you use.)

Privacy issues

Nothing is really ever private or temporary when you are online. The things you do online can be sent all over the world, time and again, and the information you reveal online can be used to trace you or commit acts of cyber bullying. There are a number of ways to protect your online identity and limit the risks involved.

Spam alert

"**Spam**" is unwanted emails from people you do not know. These can include chain email letters that you are supposed to send on to people in your address list. Sometimes these can be very nasty. One 13-year-old girl was terrified when she received an email that included a picture of a dead child with the threat that this would be her if she did not forward the email to 15 of her friends. The simple solution to these kinds of spam or threats is to delete them immediately.

Gone phishing

Phishing is when people try to fool you into revealing personal information for criminal gain. They send out a number of official-looking emails or pop-ups asking you to visit a (fake) website and enter personal or private information, such as passwords and bank account numbers. Sometimes they pretend to be well-known banks. If people take the bait, the identity thieves use their information to remove money from their bank accounts. It is quite hard to tell phishing emails or web pages from real ones. But remember that no reputable organization would ask for all that information in an email or open web page, so NEVER provide it.

Here are some tips to help you avoid email scams:

TIP

- Never open email attachments from people you do not know.
- Ask your ISP about spam and junk mail filters to block nuisance mails.
- Do not click on any links in spam emails you receive. You do not know where you will end up, and it could make your computer vulnerable to viruses.
- Never forward spam on to your friends, even if chain emails promise great money rewards or contain threats.

 Think carefully before you let someone take photos of you with a cell phone. They can be changed and shared very easily. Once it is out there, anyone can see it!

If you are going into a new chatroom or blog site, make sure you choose nicknames and screen names carefully.

Getting it Right

Web experts recommend that you create a unique password or screen name that has a mixture of letters and numbers, and that does not give any important information away. For example, never use your birth date or street name as a password, and try not to indicate whether you are male or female.

Online gaming

Online gaming allows you to create new identities in a virtual world or take part in adventures with people on the other side of the world. Online gaming risks include meeting strangers who may trick you into revealing your personal or financial details.

Another hazard can be viruses and other nuisance programs hidden in game files that you can download. However, using a computer security system such as a **firewall** should guard against these viruses.

Online gambling is big business worldwide. But don't be tempted by the lure of fast money. Most of the time, the only people who become rich are the owners of the gaming sites.

Gambling

Gambling on the Internet has become increasingly popular. Although teenagers can only legally play for free and without any risk of losing real money, there are other risks.

Think about why gambling sites would offer you free games in the first place. Free sites can be fun, but they can also encourage you to develop an **addiction** to gambling. After a while, you may be tempted to start gambling for real money as soon as (or even before) you are legally old enough to do so.

The problem with this is twofold: first, underage gambling is against the law; second, you could become addicted to gambling for life. Not only would this put you at risk of being cheated by con artists, but it could lead to serious debt and untold misery in the future.

It is possible to become addicted to being online. As a result, people may find themselves isolated from friends and family, and this can lead to depression. To stop this from happening to you, make sure you develop other interests and spend time doing other things with friends. If you play online games too often and for too long, without taking regular breaks, you also risk repetitive strain injury to your hands and wrists. In South Korea the average high school student spends 23 hours per week gaming online, and the country considers Internet addiction a major public health issue!

Getting it
Wrong

ARE YOU AN ONLINE ADDICT?

Answer this quiz to find out if you are addicted to the Internet. Then turn to page 50 for the verdict.

- Do you think about your online games or conversations during the rest of the day and plan your next online session?

- Do you find you have to spend more and more time online before you have had enough?

- Have you tried before to control or cut back on your Internet time but failed?

- Do you feel restless, moody, or irritable when you miss a couple of days or more of Internet use?

- Do you frequently stay online longer than you planned or than you know you should?

- Have you missed out on something important like a great day out or failed to turn in important school assignments because of the Internet?

- Have you lied to people about how much time you spend online?

- Do you often go online to escape from problems, such as feelings of anxiety?

Under Pressure

During certain times in your life you face a lot of pressure—pressure to fit in, to please other people, to do or try things you feel unhappy about. Some pressures are normal and possibly useful, like the stress you feel before taking a test or rehearsing your lines for a show. Other pressures— such as the pressure to look right, try drugs, or join a gang—can be more risky.

UNHEALTHY EATING

Some people try to alter the way they look by dieting. This is fine if the diet is for health reasons and is followed sensibly. However, strict dieting can sometimes result in an eating disorder. **Anorexia** is a condition in which people eat so little that they may end up starving themselves. It is a serious illness, and, in the worst cases, can result in death. **Bulimia** is an equally serious condition in which people "binge eat" huge quantities of food and then get rid of the food by vomiting or taking laxatives. Anorexics and bulimics risk serious, long-term damage to their health. If you think you or someone you know has an eating disorder, get help as fast as you can. (Check out the websites and helplines at the end of this book.)

Getting it Wrong

Smoking is a risk that your body can do without. One in ten of the chemicals in cigarettes is carcinogenic (cause cancer), which is why long-term smoking can kill you. Some people seem to think smoking is cool, but they are seriously mistaken. Smoking will leave you with smelly clothes and hair, stained teeth, bad breath, a hacking cough, and dry, wrinkled skin. It is also so expensive that you won't have much money left for anything else. So, no—not cool at all!

Bodywise

You may be sick of hearing about the importance of a healthy diet and getting a good night's sleep, but these things make a real difference. It is worth remembering that regularly getting enough sleep and eating a decent diet makes you look good, feel good, and ensures you have enough energy to fit in all the things you want to do in your day. Without nine or ten hours of sleep every night, teenagers might find they have problems concentrating, which can affect schoolwork. They may also find themselves less able to deal with emotional problems and become easily depressed.

Body art

Tattoos and body piercings have become very popular, but before you rush out to get some, be aware of the risks. Both tattooing and piercing involve breaking the skin. If unsterile needles have been used, you risk infection with some serious diseases, including **HIV**. Also, think about how much your style or tastes have changed in the past few years. Will you still want to be covered in serpents and skulls when you are older?

We all know it is unfair, but appearances do count. You may risk not getting the job you want if a future employer does not like your body piercings and tattoos.

33

THE DEAL WITH DRUGS

Drugs change the way your body works. Whether injected, snorted, or swallowed, once drugs are in your bloodstream they travel around your body and reach your brain, where they basically intensify or dull your senses and make you feel high or relaxed. The problem is they can also create **hallucinations**, affect your sight, coordination, and speech, make you unconscious or unable to move, or, in the worst cases, even kill you.

The risks

When you are a teenager, your body is growing and going through massive changes as you develop into an adult. Taking drugs can have long-lasting consequences. It may be true that one hit won't usually kill you, but using drugs (and alcohol and tobacco) when you are young increases the risk of becoming addicted. In addition to the serious health problems addiction brings, addicts also end up detached from the world by dropping out of activities they used to love, often becoming angry and aggressive over

In an ideal world it should be easy for you to say "no" to drugs or alcohol—and have that totally accepted, without being made to feel uncool, or "chicken." However, in the real world it is often not so easy. If you feel the need to back up your refusal to take drugs or alcohol with a good reason, try one of these:

* Say you have homework, an important sports game, or a test to take the next day and you cannot risk messing it up.

* Say you are sick and don't want to get even worse and ruin everyone else's evening.

* Lie and say you have tried it before and became really sick. Your doctor suspects that you have a dangerous allergy to it.

* Say that your parents have threatened to stop your allowance and ground you for a month if you go home high or drunk.

* Say you recently met someone with a drug or drinking problem and there is no way you want to go down that road.

TIP

nothing. Drug users can lose friends and confidence, and when they start to miss school and fail their classes, they risk their chances of having a great future.

So, why do it?

It may seem that lots of people are doing drugs, but they are not, and you are not unusual or weird if you choose not to! Some people do drugs because they think that it will help them escape the stresses of the real world. In reality, drugs may temporarily alter your sense of reality, but afterward most people feel far worse and more stressed. Taking substances like drugs or alcohol makes you take more dangerous risks and may make you do something you will deeply regret later.

The simplest answer to give people who try to press you into trying alcohol or drugs is NO. You should be able to say "no" firmly and confidently and without giving any explanation. But it is not always as easy as that because some people can be really pushy. (See the Tip box on page 34 for some advice on how to deal with this.)

These two photos of the same young crystal meth addict were taken 18 months apart. It is easy to see how badly her health and looks have been damaged by the drug.

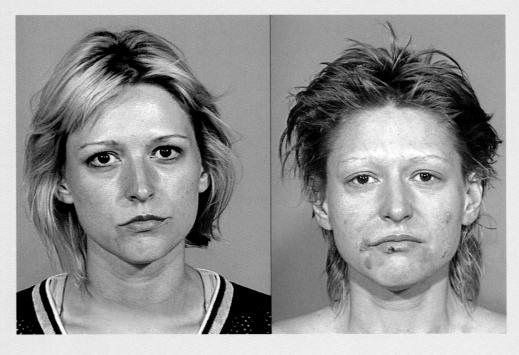

You should never keep quiet about abuse. If you are the victim of neglect, or physical or sexual abuse, it is important that you tell someone you trust as soon as you can.

If someone touches you in places that make you feel uncomfortable or hurts you, or tells you to take your clothes off when you don't want to, this is sexual abuse, and you need to tell someone you trust immediately. Remember, it is never *your* fault—no matter how friendly you have been to this person before it happened, and no matter who the person is. The person's behavior is unacceptable and must be stopped.

Getting it Right

WHAT IS ABUSE?

The temptation to abuse their own bodies with drugs, alcohol, or tobacco is not the only risk some people face. They may also suffer abuse from other people.

Physical abuse is when someone hits, punches, or otherwise hurts someone else. Sexual abuse is when someone forces sexual contact upon someone else without his or her consent. Physical and sexual abuse is always unacceptable, and particularly so when the abuser is an adult and the victim is a child or young person.

Neglect is a type of abuse, too. Neglect is when parents or caregivers either do not provide children with their physical needs, such as adequate food or medical care, or when they don't fulfill a child's emotional needs and constantly criticize, threaten, or yell at them.

The impact of abuse

In addition to the immediate effects of physical abuse, people who are or who have been abused often have trouble eating and sleeping. They may feel scared, depressed, or angry a lot of the time. They also feel cut off from friends and school life and lose all **self-esteem**.

The most important thing to recognize about abuse is that if it happens to you it is not, in any way, shape, or form, your fault or the result of anything you may or may not have done. Whatever anybody says to you or threatens you with, you are not to blame and must not risk letting the abuse continue.

Dealing with it

Never listen if abusers threaten you with trouble if you tell anyone what they have been doing. They are only saying this because they know that what they have done is terribly wrong, and they are scared of being found out. The more usual outcome of letting people know what has happened is that the abuser is never allowed to behave like that again—which can only be a good thing. If you or someone you know has been or is being abused, you must report it immediately to someone you trust—a parent, caregiver, teacher, doctor, or the police.

This is more straightforward when the abuser is a stranger, but it may be harder to do if the abuser is someone you know, especially if the person is a member of your family who treats you kindly most of the time. However, you have to go through with it—to reduce the risk to yourself, to other people who might also be harmed, and also to the abusers themselves, so that they can get the help they need to sort out their problem.

You can get free, confidential help from a variety of different organizations (see page 53 for some suggestions). They can advise you on what you should do if you think someone you know is being abused.

BAD Behavior

Antisocial behavior is any activity that has an impact on other people in the community in a negative way. It includes letting off fireworks late at night in a quiet street, getting into fights, shoplifting, or vandalizing property. Antisocial behavior puts teens at risk because they may get hurt or get into trouble with the law. For instance, more than half of the people injured and burned by fireworks each year are under 16 years old.

When you hang out with a bad crowd, there is increased pressure to try drugs and alcohol. This makes it more likely that you will get injured in fights, because statistically alcohol and substance abuse increases the likelihood and severity of violence.

Find alternatives

Some young people end up committing petty crimes, such as vandalism, graffiti, or shoplifting, because their friends do it or because they like the buzz they get from trying something risky. Some people think these activities are not that serious, but they are all criminal offenses for which you could be arrested and end up with a criminal record.

The best way to avoid risks like these is to stay away from friends who make these mistakes, and keep busy! Find healthier and low-risk activities, such as sports, a part-time job, or a craft project.

A good example is an alternative to graffiti vandalism. Many of the kids who spray graffiti have a lot of artistic skill and talent. If they transferred those talents to canvas or wood they would have a great piece of art to hang, give to friends, or even sell for extra spending money. And they would not run the risk of having their hard work spoiled or painted over by other "graffiti artists"!

What does it give you?

If you sit down and think about it, finding something else to do that actually improves your life (such as sports or earning extra cash), or that teaches you something valuable for later life (such as an auto mechanic class, or classes to improve your computer or craft skills), has got to be better than spending your spare time on a mindless course of destruction.

Antisocial behavior gives you precisely *nothing*. It does nothing for your self-esteem, results in nothing but anger and sadness from everyone around you, puts you in danger, and may possibly leave you with a criminal record and a bad reputation that could stick with you for the rest of your life.

Knife- and gun-related crime can result in terrible tragedy.

Some young people carry knives or guns for "protection," but carrying a weapon actually increases the likelihood that you will become a

Getting it Wrong

victim of crime. If you get into an argument while carrying a weapon, you are more likely to use it. You could end up hurting or killing someone, or the weapon could be taken from you and used on you instead. You risk a heavy prison sentence if you hurt someone.

SELF-DEFENSE

When someone is angry or threatening you, the best response is not to shout or fight back, as this is only likely to make matters worse. Instead, try to defuse the situation.

For instance, if people are bullying you or trying to lure you into a fight, you can simply walk away—ideally toward a crowded place where they won't dare continue their taunts. Alternatively, you could make it appear that you agree with them until you get a chance to escape. It is also best to quietly hand over your bag to a mugger rather than struggle with them and risk getting hurt.

Getting it Right

When faced with a difficult situation, don't just follow along because you don't want to look uncool in front of your friends. Take a moment to think about what you really feel, and think about and judge the options for yourself. Trust your instincts and get out of a situation you feel uncomfortable with before anything bad can happen.

Resisting pressure

Have you ever been faced with another teenager wanting you to do something dangerous, harmful, or illegal? The first thing to remember is that you have an absolute right to be treated with respect—which means the right to refuse to do something you do not want to do without being bullied or taunted.

The best weapon to use against people who confront you or try to push you into doing something you do not want to do is assertiveness. Being assertive simply means being firm without being aggressive.

To become more assertive, the first step is to recognize that everyone has the right to say "no" and to refuse a request to do something they do not want to do without feeling guilty. So, if someone is trying to persuade you to do something you feel uncomfortable with, look the person straight in the eye and with a serious face say simply, "No, I don't want to do that."

CAN YOU DEAL WITH PEER PRESSURE?

Does peer pressure control you, or do you know your own mind? Answer "yes" or "no" to these questions and then turn to page 50 to find out what your answers mean.

1) Have you ever bought clothes or had your hair cut to look like your friends?

2) Do you pick on people just because everyone else in your group is doing it?

3) Have you ever helped a friend cheat on homework or during a test?

4) Have you ever tried cigarettes or alcohol at a party or with friends because everyone else was doing it?

5) Have you ever joined a club or team you weren't particularly interested in, to be with a friend?

6) Have you ever lied to your parents to be with friends or because friends told you to?

7) Have you ever done anything you later regretted just to make somebody like you?

8) Have you ever done something physically risky or illegal because others were doing it?

9) Do you sometimes get talked into doing things that you regret later?

10) Have your friends ever talked you into doing something illegal or harmful?

If The Worst Happens ...

An emergency is a sudden and unexpected crisis that threatens people or property and requires immediate attention. By its very nature an emergency is something you cannot really plan for, but there are precautions you can take. You should also know some of the safety procedures used in an emergency, just in case you ever need to use them.

Be Prepared

When you are in charge of a house, either at home or babysitting at someone else's home, you should be prepared. To start with, your parents should know where you are, and you should know how to get in touch with them at all times. You should also have a list of local emergency services and telephone numbers of adults you can call if anything goes wrong. It is also important to make sure the house is secure, so lock all the doors and windows.

Never open the door for someone you don't know. If the phone rings, never let a caller know that no one is home. Simply say that your parents are busy and take a message.

In case of fire

The best preparation for fire is to reduce the risk of having one in the first place. Be very careful when using candles, lighters, or matches, and never leave them unattended. When you are cooking, remember to

Getting it Right

To reduce the risk of being trapped or injured by fire, every home should be fitted with smoke alarms that make a loud beeping noise when they sense smoke.

- There should be smoke alarms on every floor of a house, especially by bedrooms.

- Test smoke alarms monthly to make sure they are working.

- Replace old batteries with new ones at least once a year.

Never throw water onto a grease fire. If possible, slide the lid back on top of the pan (using an oven mitt).

use a timer so you don't forget what is cooking. Remember to switch off appliances after using them.

Get your family to discuss and plan an escape route that you can all use in case of fire. Fires can burn fast and smoke can make a home very dark, so you should all know where the fire escapes or exits are located in case you need to use them. This is especially important in a house with two storeys or more.

TIP

The kitchen can be a dangerous place, so follow these tips to keep safe.

- Turn pot handles so that they are not sticking out over the edge of the stovetop.
- Use a heatproof trivet for putting hot pots and pans on.
- Use a potholder or oven mitts to handle hot pans.
- Keep clothes away from stoves so they do not catch fire.
- Be very careful with sharp knives.

Who to call in an emergency

If you find yourself or someone else in danger, you should dial 911 immediately. You can call from any phone at no charge—calls to emergency numbers are free. The number gets you through to an operator who will link you up with whichever of the different emergency services you need—the fire department, ambulance service, police, or the coastguards.

If you are not sure which service you need, the 911 operator will help you decide before putting you through to the right emergency service. Another operator will then ask for more details.

Getting it Wrong

While it is absolutely right to call emergency numbers in a real emergency, in many countries it is considered a crime to dial 911 as a joke or to ask about something minor like getting a cat out of a tree. If you take up an emergency operator's time, it could cause a delay getting help to people involved in a real emergency, and you could be responsible for a tragedy.

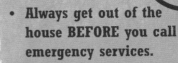

If you are involved in a fire:

- Always get out of the house **BEFORE** you call emergency services.

- Never stop to collect belongings—just get yourself and the people you are with outside fast!

- Shout "Fire" as you run to make sure everyone else in a big building is alerted.

- Feel a closed door before opening it. If it is hot, there may be fire on the other side, so get out another way.

- When escaping, stay low to the floor. Smoke rises, so the safest air to breathe is down low.

- If your clothes catch on fire, drop to the floor and roll over to put them out.

When calling emergency services, try to stay as calm as possible. The more information you can give the operator about where you are and what has happened, the better.

What to do after a collision

If you are involved in a minor road accident, the first thing to do is to check that no one (including you) is injured. You should then write down the other person's name, address, license plate number, and insurance information. You should also write down the contact details of at least two witnesses, if possible. One of the people involved in the accident should report the incident to the police—if possible, from the scene of the accident. If you have a cell phone with a camera, it is also a good idea to take pictures of the scene and jot down what happened, in case you need to explain it to the police.

You might also think about booking a visit to the doctor. Even if you do not think you are hurt, injuries sometimes show up later.

✚ FIRST AID

First aid is giving basic assistance to someone who has just been injured, or become suddenly sick, until proper medical assistance arrives. Ideally, we should all get first-aid training so that we know exactly what to do when someone is hurt. But having even a small amount of knowledge of first aid could make the difference between life and death.

TIP

If you want to train in first aid, there are a number of organizations that can help. Local branches of the Red Cross offer several classes in first-aid techniques for the public, including classes for teens. Many local community organizations and hospitals also offer opportunities to learn more about first aid.

BURNS

To deal with burns: Put the injury under cold running water for at least 10 minutes (as long as the skin is not cut), or cover it with clean, wet towels. Take off or cut away clothing or jewelry near the affected area, unless it is stuck to the burn. Do not use ice, ointments, or anything else on the wound—just put some plastic wrap or a clean pad over it.

CHOKING

If someone is choking: Hit the person firmly between the shoulder blades up to five times with the base of your hand. If this doesn't work, stand behind the person, clasp your hands together tightly just above the person's navel (belly button), and pull inward and upward. If this doesn't work, call an ambulance immediately.

BLEEDING

To deal with someone who is bleeding: Wear clean rubber gloves or put a clean plastic bag over your hand if you can. Try to stop the bleeding by putting pressure on the wound—for example, by holding your finger over the wound. Alternatively, put a clean cloth or bandage over the wound and hold it in place with a cloth strip, a belt, or even a tie.

POISONING

If someone has taken a poisonous substance: Regardless of whether the person just has a stomachache or is throwing up, call a doctor or ambulance immediately. While you are waiting for help, stay with the person and find out as much as you can about what he or she took, and how much. Keep the bottle or container with you to help the medics.

• CHECKLIST •

THE RECOVERY POSITION

If you are present when someone has had an accident or has been pulled out of water, and seems to be unconscious, you can help by putting the person in the recovery position.

- First check that airways (breathing tubes) are clear, and there is nothing in the mouth to stop breathing. Place the person on his or her back, tilt the head back, and lift the chin. To check breathing, watch, listen, and feel the person's chest.

- The person's arm nearest to you should be positioned at a right angle to his or her body, with the elbow bent and palm facing upward.

- Lift the person's other arm toward you, over the body, and gently roll the person toward you onto his or her side. Position this arm across the body, with the hand tucked under the cheek.

- Adjust the person's uppermost leg, so that the knee is bent at a right angle and touching the ground in front of the body, with the foot flat on the ground.

- Tilt the person's head back to ensure that the airway is open.

- Call emergency services for immediate help.

IMPORTANT NOTE: You should NEVER move someone if you suspect he or she may have a back or neck injury.

AFTERCARE

When you have been through a crisis, accident, or trauma of any kind, you may find that the emotional damage takes longer to get over than any physical damage. In most cases, it is wrong to ignore the incident or to try to pretend that it never happened to you; instead it is better to talk about it. You could either talk to friends or family, or you could consider seeing a **counselor** or **therapist**. These are trained, qualified professionals who help others work through their problems or issues.

Seeking help from professionals for stress, addiction, or emotional difficulties is not a sign of weakness. There is no difference between seeing a counselor and seeing a doctor for a physical illness. The degree of importance is the same—you need help as soon as possible to sort out a problem that is affecting your life.

Change your ways

Counselors and therapists can also help you deal with addictions to cigarettes, alcohol, or drugs, or to control and stop other risky kinds of behavior. Counselors or advisers will not tell you what to do or judge you. They will ask you how you would like things to be different and encourage you to suggest ideas of how you could change your behavior. Then they will help you find ways to make those changes a reality.

How counseling works

Most people have a meeting with their counselor or therapist once a week or every two weeks, either alone or with parents. During the sessions the counselor may ask you questions about the main problem in your life, but you can also feel free to talk about anything that is on your mind. You can continue going to sessions with your counselor for however long you feel you need to work through your problems.

TIP

If you think you would like to talk to a counselor or therapist, you can ask your parent or caregiver to help you find one. Your doctor can recommend one, or you can ask a teacher, school nurse, youth advisor, or religious leader.

Sometimes it is easier to discuss all your feelings honestly with someone who does not know your friends and family, but who can still understand and is experienced in helping people with similar difficulties.

Along with talking things through with your counselor, there are a number of things you can do to help yourself through tough times. You might try writing down your feelings in a journal or diary, or try relaxation exercises, listening to music, or exercising. When you are finding life tough, it is important to continue doing the things that you enjoy. So, play basketball, watch a movie, read a book, and spend time with your friends—anything that makes you smile.

Getting it Right

QUIZ RESULTS

ANSWERS FOR QUIZ ON PAGE 15

1) False—there is no band on Earth worth losing your hearing for.
2) False—in some ways you are more likely to get injured when you are inexperienced, so everyone who plays a sport should wear the recommended safety gear.
3) True
4) True
5) True
6) False—polluted water contains disease-causing microorganisms, which can enter the body through the ears, eyes, nose, mouth, or through broken skin.
7) False—avoid the sun at the peak of the day, between 11 am and 3 pm.
8) False—always swim with friends so they can call for help if you get into unexpected difficulties.
9) Obviously false! Warming up means stretching and loosening your muscles to prepare them for a serious workout!

ANSWERS FOR QUIZ ON PAGE 21

All As: Congratulations! You know what you are doing. Just make sure that you always put into practice what you know.

All Bs: You are not totally lacking in street sense, but you need to read some safety advice more carefully.

All Cs: You should not be allowed out of the house without a chaperone!

ANSWERS FOR QUIZ ON PAGE 31

If you answered "yes" to five or more of the questions in this quiz, you are probably spending too much time glued to your screen and may even have an addiction to the Internet or online gaming. Try to gradually cut down on the number of hours you spend at the screen—perhaps even setting an alarm clock to remind you when your time is up. Make a promise to yourself that you will go out with friends regularly, exercise more, and that you will rejoin that sports team or band you left. As you gradually regain a social life, you will start to enjoy being part of the real world more and more and will not be so reliant on the virtual world.

ANSWERS FOR QUIZ ON PAGE 41

Mostly "yes": You tend to do what your friends do and rarely stand up for yourself. The problem is that this probably leaves you feeling bad, which makes you less self-confident and even more likely to follow other people. Now is the time to change. You know when something feels wrong, so speak up for yourself and do what you think is best. It will feel good and give you new confidence and self-respect.

Mostly "no": You are likely to keep safe because you are smart! You are confident enough to stand your ground against peer pressure and do not follow the crowd. You have a strong sense of what is right and wrong and you are unlikely to let anyone pull you in the wrong direction.

About half "yes" and half "no": You manage to think for yourself and do the right thing most of the time. When you don't, it is probably because you don't really know where you stand on an issue, so you just go with the flow. The best thing to do is trust your instincts. If something inside you says no, go with that—you don't have to explain your decision; you just have to go with it.

(20) THINGS TO REMEMBER

1 Take positive risks! It is important to be safe, but as long as you take precautions and make sensible choices, no one is saying you should never try sky-diving or white-water rafting!

2 Think about the potential dangers in a situation, but don't make yourself scared. The chances of something bad happening to you are low, but it pays to be aware of the risks involved.

3 Take your time. Don't rush into making a decision. Assess the risks and think about why you might do something.

4 Be assertive. Learn how to stand your ground firmly and convincingly—and without anger.

5 Make sure you have and wear the right gear for any sports you play.

6 Get organized. Being safe is about thinking ahead. How will you get back from that party? If you are cycling, do you need bike lights?

7 Trust your instincts. If it feels wrong, say "no" right away.

8 Be streetwise. Avoid traveling alone if you can. Don't let pride prevent you from calling out for help if you need it.

9 If you get a part-time job, check out what permits you need and what hours you can work.

10 If in doubt, talk it out. Learn from other people's experiences.

11 If someone bothers you online, log off. Create a new screen name and start over.

12 Keep parents and caregivers informed about where you are and who you are with.

13 Don't take chances on the road. Wear your seat belt and only get rides from responsible drivers. Anything else just isn't worth the risk.

14 Take care of your body. You only have one to last you a lifetime.

15 Avoid cigarettes, drugs, and alcohol. There are far better ways of spending your cash.

16 Walk away from trouble. The best thing to do when someone is being aggressive or trying to fight with you is to leave the situation.

17 Learn some basic first-aid skills. They could save someone's life—or even your own.

18 Try not to flash cash or belongings around. Keep valuables and purses covered and stowed away safely when you are out.

19 Keep emergency phone numbers on you at all times and, if you can, carry a cell phone. Check that it is fully charged before you go out so that you can always get help if you need it.

20 Talk about it! If something happens to you that harms you or makes you unhappy, tell someone about it and get help. That is the only way that things will change.

Further Information

BOOKS

Fitzhugh, Karla, Jane Bingham, and Suzanna Drew-Edwards. *What's the Deal?* (10-book series on drug abuse and addiction). Chicago: Heinemann Library, 2006.

Gedatus, Gus. *Travel Safety* (*Perspectives on Violence*). Mankato, Minn.: LifeMatters, 2000.

Haugen, Hayley Mitchell, and Susan Musser, eds. *Internet Safety* (*Issues That Concern You*). Detroit: Greenhaven, 2008.

Willard, Nancy E. *Cyber-Safe Kids, Cyber-Savvy Teens: Helping Young People Learn to Use the Internet Safely and Responsibly*. San Francisco: Jossey Bass, 2007.

WEBSITES

http://kidshealth.org/teen/safety/safebasics/internet_safety.html
This website offers tips for safe surfing on the Internet for young people.

www.chatdanger.com
This website has tips for keeping safe in chatrooms and other interactive services online.

http://endabuse.org/section/programs/teens
This website offers guidance and help for abused teenagers.

http://kidshealth.org/teen/safety/safebasics/bike_safety.html
Learn more about cycling safety at this website.

ORGANIZATIONS

Childhelp
www.childhelp.org/get_help
The Childhelp National Child Abuse Hotline is a free 24-hour helpline for young people. You can call the helpline at 1-800-4-A-CHILD (1-800-422-4453) about problems related to abuse or neglect at any time, day or night. Counselors are there to help you find ways to sort things out. Find out more on the website.

National Eating Disorders Association
www.nationaleatingdisorders.org
The National Eating Disorders Association is an organization aimed at educating people about eating disorders and offering support to those who are affected. To get help, call the helpline at 1-800-931-2237.

Crimestoppers
www.crimestopusa.com
Crimestoppers is an organization aimed at putting criminals behind bars through an anonymous free phone number: 1-800-245-0009.

National Center for Victims of Crime
www.ncvc.org
The National Center for Victims of Crime is an organization that gives free and confidential help to anyone who has been affected by crime. People there provide practical information and will also help you get counseling if you feel you need it. Call 1-800-FYI-CALL (1-800-394-2255).

American Red Cross
www.redcross.org/SERVICES/HSS/courses/
The Red Cross offers first-aid training courses. Its Babysitter's Training is designed specifically for teens. Visit the website to find out more.

GLOSSARY

addiction physical dependence on something

anorexia eating disorder involving loss of appetite for food, severe weight loss, and muscle wasting

antisocial behavior acting in a way that causes harassment, alarm, or distress to other people

blog online diary or journal in which people can post messages for others to see and respond to

bulimia eating disorder in which a person binges (eats large amounts of food) and then vomits or uses laxatives to get rid of it in order to prevent weight gain

cancer abnormal, uncontrolled growth of cells in any part of the body, which can spread to surrounding or distant organs and can cause death

chatroom site on the Internet where a number of users can have an online conversation

cool-down short period of gentle exercise such as slow running or jogging done after a workout or competition to loosen muscles

copyright law that protects an original artistic or literary work

counselor someone who gives advice about problems

decibel level measure of the intensity or loudness of a sound

entrepreneur person who takes the risk of organizing and operating a new business venture

firewall computer system that prevents unauthorized access to or from a private network

hallucination when a person sees, hears, smells, tastes, or feels something that is not really there

HIV stands for "human immunodeficiency virus." It is the virus that causes AIDS. It is passed from one person to the other through infected blood and body fluids.

instant messenger (IM) service that allows users to send and receive short messages instantly via the Internet

Internet service provider (ISP) company that provides Internet access for a fee

peer someone who is your equal—for example, is the same age as you

phishing email scam used to persuade people to disclose personal information, such as passwords

plagiarism taking someone else's work or ideas and pretending they are your own

reflective material that reflects, or bounces back, light (such as a mirror)

self-esteem sense of self-worth, of feeling pleased with and confident in yourself

spam unwelcome and uninvited emails on the Internet; also known as junk mail

spyware program or software that secretly gathers information about a user while he or she uses the Internet

strain injury to a muscle in which the muscle fibers tear as a result of overstretching

supervision when someone watches over workers, including trainees, to ensure safety regulations are followed

therapist person who treats people for problems, such as emotional problems

vandalism needlessly destroying other people's or public property

virus program intended to cause mischief or damage to a computer system

warm-up running and stretching done before exercise or sports to gradually warm up the body for more intense training or racing

Index